*For my love – Stuart,
and our beautiful family*

Published by Love Menu™
PO Box 1022
Ulladulla NSW 2539
lovemenu@bigpond.com
First published in 2010
Printed in China by
EVERBEST PRINTING CO LTD
Website: www.everbest.com
Copyright Love Menu™ 2010

All rights reserved.
No part of this publication may be reproduced, stored in a retrieval system, or transmitted, in any form or by any means, electronic, mechanical photocopying, recording or otherwise without the prior written permission of the copyright owner and the publisher.

www.lovemenu.com.au

A special thank you to Andrew Peace Wines for helping make this project a reality.

Foreword

Romantic by name, romantic by nature.

Cooking with romantic ingredients such as; roses, flowers, champagne and more, to create a unique dining experience for all seasons where 'love' is on the menu for entree, main and dessert.

There is also a special occasion menu for particular dates of importance in the calendar including Valentine's Day, your wedding anniversary or any significant event whether it be it just for love, or a special time of the season.

Though the seasons may change, as will the menu, love always remains, for "love is not a seasonal thing".

All dishes have been paired up with wine from Andrew Peace Wines – which I like to refer to as 'Love and Peace'.

I have enjoyed a long-standing relationship with the Peace family, and have learned that the matching of food and wine enhances the overall dining experience, helping to complement the flavours and aromas of the dishes prepared.

Live with Peace in your heart, and share the love … and the wine … with your friends. Isn't that what it's all about?

Contents:

Summer menu	7
Autumn menu	29
Winter menu	51
Spring menu	73
Special occasion menu	96
Special date menu	97
Valentine's menu	97
Wedding/anniversary menu	97
Andrew Peace Wines	118 - 120
Wild Hibiscus Flower Company	120
Index	120

"There's love in all cooking."
— Anonymous

Summer menu

December
E: Roasted champagne oysters
M: Parcel of chicken & champagne
D: Champagne & flowers sorbet

January
E: Rosette of fish
M: Quail in a bed of roses
D: Poached pears in champagne

February
E: Love all the thyme in Vienna with roasted garlic & fetta
M: In love with fish & chips
D: Golden syrup love dumplings

Roasted champagne oysters

Ingredients:
4 oysters
4 bacon rashers
dipping sauce:
118ml champagne or sparkling wine
1 tsp dijon mustard
1 tsp lemon juice
2 egg yolks
125g cubed butter
salt and white pepper

Method:
1. Remove the eye of the bacon rasher and wrap it to imitate a lily so that it may hold an oyster and use a toothpick to secure it.
2. Cut the rest of the bacon to be a long strip in length and even in width.
3. Wrap the length of bacon around a metal rod or some aluminium foil rolled up to imitate a rod.
4. Roast bacon for about 7-10 minutes at 180°C in a fan forced oven, or until almost cooked.
5. Remove from rod and it should retain its form. Insert oyster in eye of bacon and roast for a further 5 minutes, so that the bacon becomes crispy and the oyster warmed through.

Dipping sauce:
1. Prepare dipping sauce when bacon goes into the oven. Start by placing a heatproof bowl over simmering water and place champagne in bowl, reduce by about half and then set aside to cool a little.
2. Place heatproof bowl with champagne back over simmering water. Add two egg yolks and whisk until paler in colour and liquid becomes very warm. Be careful not to boil liquid.
3. Add mustard and lemon juice and whisk in. Add salt and pepper.
4. Add the softened cubed butter, whisking it in one cube at a time. Mixture should thicken, then take off heat. Serve.

Drink with this...
Sparkling Chardonnay Pinot

"Toasted yeasty notes and a creamy texture. Classic dry, fully matured, elegant sparkling wine with distinctive characters and a gentle, flowery bouquet. A great sparkling wine for celebrations and seafood."

Parcel of chicken & champagne

Ingredients:
1 small onion
2 bacon rashers chopped
1 large chicken breast sliced
1 teaspoon crushed garlic
5 sheets filo pastry
2 teaspoons cracked pepper
300ml thickened cream
400ml champagne or sparkling wine
1 sheet puff pastry
*Can be served with a side of salad or vegetables

Method:
1. Marinate chicken in the champagne or sparkling wine for two hours.
2. Gently saute onion and bacon and set aside.
3. In a seperate pan, seal chicken and then add to the onion and bacon and add all other ingredients, mixing well. Take off heat and set aside.
4. Set fan forced oven to 175°C. Cut puff pastry into two lots of 6cm squares and bake until golden (about 5-10 minutes).
5. Take 5 sheets of filo pastry and brush melted butter between each layer and place on top of each other. Cut the layered filo pastry into two large square portions.
6. Place cooked puff pastry in the centre of each of the filo pastry squares.
7. Divide the chicken mixture into 2 portions and place on top of puff pastry square.
8. Take each corner of the filo pastry and bring together at the top, scrunching the pastry together.
9. Bake for 10-15 minutes or until golden.

Drink with this...
Chardonnay

"A lovely crisp wine, elegant and bristling with tropical fruit flavours. Not heavily oaked so it's great for drinking chilled, on its own. It's also worth trying with fresh fish and grilled chicken salads."

Champagne & flowers sorbet

Ingredients:
1 cup raspberries
1/2 cup water
2 tbs lemon juice
2 egg whites
2 tbs wild hibiscus syrup
2 wild hibiscus flowers
1/2 cup caster sugar
1 cup champagne

Method:
1. Boil champagne in a pot and add sugar. Stir until dissolved and simmer for two minutes, then stand.
2. Blend raspberries, water, lemon, egg whites, syrup and flowers.
3. Slowly add champagne mixture and blend for a further 5-10 minutes.
4. Strain through a tea towel. You may need to twist the tea towel and press out the mixture.
5. Blend again for a few minutes.
6. Place in a metal or glass bowl and freeze, making sure to stir with a fork every hour. Allow to set overnight.
7. Serve in a glass of ice with flowers.*

* To make the glass of ice with flowers, simply get a coffee mug and place some flowers and leaves in the bottom. Then place a small ramekin inside. (It should be a neat fit but still allow small flowers to be placed between the ramekin and the mug). Fill the mug with water, but not the ramekin, and then freeze. To turn out the glass of ice, submerge the mug in warm water and place some warm water in the ramekin.

Drink with this...

Peace in my soul White

"A little sweet and a little bubbly, just like you! Live with Peace in your soul, and share the enlightenment... and the wine... with your friends. Isn't that what it's all about?"

Rosette of fish

Ingredients:
1 trussed tomato
1 fillet of Basa
(halved to make two long thin fillets)
1 small red chilli
1 clove garlic
25g butter
1 tsp chopped thyme
1 cucumber
salt
white pepper

Method:
1. Halve the fillets to make two long and thin fillets.
2. Finely slice tomato and layer over the fillets.
3. Season with salt and pepper. Roll up and place on skewer.
4. Melt butter in pan and add chopped chilli, garlic and thyme.
5. Place fish on aluminium foil, adding one tablespoon of butter mixture on top. Seal foil, being careful not to pierce with skewer.
6. Place in a fan forced oven at 200°C, for 10-15 minutes, or until cooked.
7. Serve on top of finely sliced cucumber, with a little butter drizzled on top and skewer removed.

Drink with this...
Pinot Grigio

"The palate is full, comprising a richness akin to the variety. With a clean lime and grapefruit crispness, it is complemented by the tropical fruit nuances. Best with salad and seafood."

Quail in a bed of roses

Ingredients:
4 large red roses
1 teaspoon crushed garlic
1 teaspoon sugar
3/4 cup chicken stock
3/4 cup red wine
1/2 teaspoon arrowroot
2 quail

cous cous:
1/2 tsp crushed garlic
1/4 tsp chilli powder
1/2 cup chicken stock
1/2 cup cous cous
1 tbs olive oil
*Can be served with a side of salad or vegetables

Method:
1. Combine all ingredients for cous cous and let stand for one hour to absorb the liquid.
2. Set fan forced oven to 180°C.
3. Stuff quail with cous cous. You may need some cooking twine to hold the legs in place and some toothpicks.
4. Place the quail in an ovenproof fry pan and place in the oven for 20-25 minutes.
5. While quail is in the oven, place the petals from two roses in a blender with the chicken stock, arrowroot, sugar and crushed garlic. Blend well and then strain through a tea towel.
6. After 20-25 minutes of the quail being in the oven, put the grill on and place the quail on a tray in the oven for a further 5 minutes to ensure the top is brown – or until golden.
7. Use the frypan to make the rose jus. Place the pan on the stovetop and add the red wine to lift the jus from the pan. Bring to the boil to cook off the alcohol. Add the mix from the blender and reduce.
8. Serve with a red rose, quail and jus.

Drink with this...
Malbec

"Positioned between robust and soft, this succulent wine is fruity with spice. The aroma has a hint of plums, cherries and raspberries. Serve with BBQ and Mediterranean cuisine."

Poached pears in champagne

Ingredients:
2 firm green pears
1 bottle of champagne or sparkling wine
1 tablespoon lemon juice
2 strips of zest of lemon
1 tablespoon pink food colouring
1/2 teaspoon cinnamon
1/4 cup wild hibiscus syrup
2 wild hibiscus flowers
1 cup caster sugar

Method:
1. Set pears and wild hibiscus flowers aside. Combine all other ingredients and bring to boil, in a small but deep pot.
2. Peel pears, leaving stem on.
3. Carefully lower the pears into the liquid and simmer for 15 minutes.
4. Remove from pot and place on cutting board.
5. Make vertical incisions 1cm apart all the way around the pear.
6. Core the pear.
7. Fan out the pear, and place a wild hibiscus flower over the stem to serve.

Drink with this...
Sparkling Chardonnay Pinot

"*Toasted yeasty notes and a creamy texture. Classic dry, fully matured, elegant sparkling wine with distinctive characters and a gentle, flowery bouquet. A great sparkling wine for celebrations and seafood.*"

Love all the thyme in Vienna with roasted garlic & fetta

Ingredients:
2 whole heads of garlic
1 Vienna loaf
1/2 tsp thyme
1/4 cup extra virgin olive oil

fetta:
1/2 tsp thyme
180g fetta
1/2 tsp chives
1/8 cup extra virgin olive oil
1/8 cup canola oil
1/2 tsp cracked black pepper
1/2 tsp chopped chilli

Method:
1. Cut the tops off the heads of garlic and wrap in aluminium foil.
2. Place in a fan forced oven at 180°C for 40 minutes.
3. Mix olive oil with thyme and brush on cut pieces of Vienna.
4. Cut fetta into small cubes and marinate with thyme, chives, oils, and peppers.
5. Toast each side of Vienna, and serve with roasted garlic and fetta*.

*To eat: Squeeze the bottom of the garlic to make the roasted garlic rise to the top. Use a knife to spread this on the Vienna and then top with fetta.

Drink with this...
Semillon Sauvignon Blanc

"Medium bodied with tropical fruit character from the Sauvignon Blanc component whilst the Semillon oozes vibrant lemon. The acidic taste works in favour with salads having oily type dressing and is perfect with fish."

In love with fish & chips

Ingredients:
2 Basa fillets halved to make long thin fillets
4 large kipfler potatoes
plain flour for dusting
1 litre of oil for frying

batter:
1 stubby imported beer
1 egg
2 cups SR flour
24 ice cubes
*Can be served with a side of salad or vegetables and - of course - lemon and/or tartare sauce

Method:
1. Peel potatoes and cut in the shape of a very long triangle. Carve into a heart shape and then oil them so they don't brown.
2. Heat oil for frying and when hot place in potatoes. Cook until golden and place in moderate oven, to keep them warm while battering and cooking the fish.
3. Place flour in a large mixing bowl and make well in centre and mix in egg and beer. Place ice cubes in batter.
4. Dust fish with flour, then dip fish through batter and place in hot oil, cooking until golden. Serve fish with chips and side dish.

Drink with this...
Sparkling Chardonnay Pinot

"Toasted yeasty notes and a creamy texture. Classic dry, fully matured, elegant sparkling wine with distinctive characters and a gentle, flowery bouquet. A great sparkling wine for celebrations and seafood."

Golden syrup love dumplings

Ingredients:
1/2 cup SR flour
20g butter
1 egg

syrup:
20g butter
1/2 cup caster sugar
1 1/2 cups water
2 tbs golden syrup
*Can be served with cream and/or ice-cream.

Method:
1. Place all ingredients for syrup in a small pot on stovetop and bring to the boil.
2. Mix ingredients for dumplings and divide into four.
3. Mould dumplings into heart shapes and place two in the boiling mixture.
4. Cook in boiling mixture for 10 minutes. (Turn the dumplings a few times to ensure they cook evenly. Use a tablespoon to continually spoon the syrup over the dumplings to ensure they remain moist).

Drink with this...
Riesling

"*Enjoy at the end of a meal or any occasion. A light bodied, refreshing and easy drinking sweet wine with a hint of pear and a clean crisp finish.*"

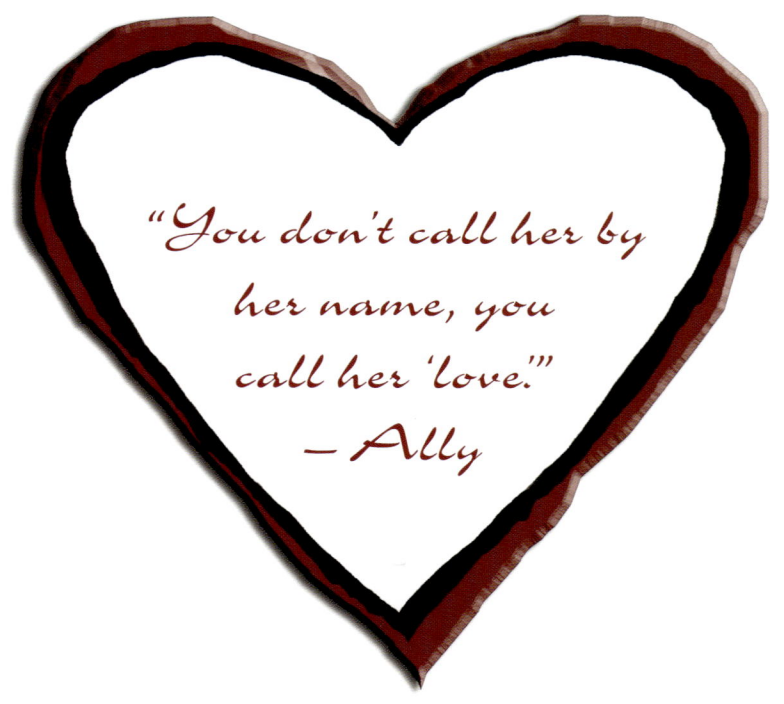

"You don't call her by her name, you call her 'love.'"
— Ally

Autumn menu

March
- E: Fettish salad
- M: Hearty chicken with potato rose
- D: Fruit of passion meringue

April
- E: Sweet pepper lamb tart
- M: Bow tie pasta with amoroso tomato
- D: Melted heart chocolate pudding

May
- E: Zucchini cakes & flower salad
- M: Duck a la rose
- D: Rosewater & white chocolate mousse

Fettish salad

Ingredients:
rocket
1 small red onion chopped
2 trussed tomatoes chopped
1 avocado diced
1 tbs olive oil
1 breadstick
balsamic vinegar for presentation
olive oil for presentation

Fettish:
300g Greek yoghurt
1 tsp cracked pepper
1 tsp crushed garlic
1 tsp chopped chives
1 tsp chopped thyme
3 green olives finely chopped
1 tsp chilli powder

Method:
1. For fettish, mix together: yoghurt, pepper, 1/2 tsp crushed garlic, chives, thyme and olives.
2. Place a tea towel over a colander and place yoghurt on top to strain.
3. Cover the top with the tea towel, occasionally pressing down to help release the liquid from the yoghurt. Do so for 4 hours, then refrigerate overnight.
4. Slice breadstick and baste with olive oil and grill.
5. In a small bowl, place diced avocado, tomato and onion, and mix well.
6. In a separate bowl, mix together 1/2 teaspoon garlic with chilli and 1 tablespoon oil.
7. Strain oil with a fork, and drizzle this over the rocket.
8. Place two large pieces of toasted Vienna on plate, top with avocado mix and then rocket.
9. Mould fettish into a flat shape 2cm in depth and cut into the shape of a heart.
10. Make a small well in the centre of the heart shape, and place what was left after straining the garlic and chilli in the centre. Serve.

Drink with this...

Semillon Sauvignon Blanc

"Medium bodied with tropical fruit character from the Sauvignon Blanc component whilst the Semillon oozes vibrant lemon. The acidic taste works in favour with salads having oily type dressing and is perfect with fish."

Hearty chicken with potato rose

Ingredients:
2 x 200g chicken fillets
100g fetta cheese
6 marinated small whole peppers
Spinach leaves
2 marinated artichoke hearts
2 potatoes
2 slices prosciutto
4 tbs oil
1 tbs butter
*Can be served with a side of salad or vegetables

Method:
1. Take each chicken fillet and slice halfway through the middle to create an opening.
2. Halve the fetta cheese to form one long strip of cheese.
3. Take three whole peppers. Cut both ends of one, and slide the fetta cheese through the middle of the pepper and then place the other two peppers on each end.
4. Place cheese and peppers inside the chicken, and press it into the chicken.
5. Slice an artichoke heart in quarters, and place inside chicken.
6. Place baby spinach over the filling, then close the chicken and secure with skewer or tooth picks.
7. Place oil in a hot pan and seal.
8. Remove skewer or toothpick and then wrap in prosciutto.
9. Cut a potato heart* and brush with melted butter.
*Peel potato. Cut a small round base and continue to peel the potato as you would an apple to create a long peel. Wind up the potato peel and place on round base of potato. Secure with a toothpick.
10. Bake chicken and potato at 175°C in a fan forced oven for 20 minutes or until cooked.
11. Serve with a garnish of baby spinach and potato rose on top.

Drink with this...
Chardonnay

"A lovely crisp wine, elegant and bristling with tropical fruit flavours. Not heavily oaked so it's great for drinking chilled, on its own. It's also worth trying with fresh fish and grilled chicken salads."

Fruit of passion meringue

Ingredients:
1 punnet strawberries
1 punnet blueberries
1 punnet raspberries
2 passionfruit
2 kiwi fruit
2 apricots
50g raspberry jam
400ml cream
2 egg whites
1/3 cup caster sugar
1/3 cup icing sugar
1/4 tsp rosewater
1/4 tsp vanilla essence

Method:
1. Whip cream and place in fridge.
2. In a clean bowl, beat egg white until firm peaks form and then slowly add caster sugar, icing sugar, essence and rosewater, beating until thick and glossy and it holds its form.
3. Pipe into small peaked shapes with a 3-4cm circumference, on a greased and lightly dusted tray.
4. Bake in a fan forced oven for 2 1/2 hours at 50°C and then turn off oven and leave meringues in the oven for a further hour.
5. Slice kiwi fruit and apricots and halve strawberries.
6. Make a circle of raspberry jam in the centre of serving plate.
7. Spoon out passionfruit and place around outside of jam.
8. Pipe whipped cream to form a high mound in centre.
9. Border with strawberries, and place meringues on top.
10. Decorate with kiwi fruit, apricots, blueberries and raspberries and dust with icing sugar.

Drink with this...
Sparkling Moscato

"Take the time to sprite your senses with an apricot tingle sensation. If that isn't sufficient combine some honeysuckle. A great combination to all celebrations and moments worth remembering."

Sweet pepper lamb tart

Ingredients:
- 1 sheet butter puff pastry
- 1 lamb shank
- 1 red capsicum
- 50g fetta
- 1 small onion
- 2 trussed tomatoes
- 1/2 tsp crushed garlic
- 1 bayleaf
- 1 slice bacon
- 1/4 cup red wine
- 1 tbs tomato paste
- 1 cup water
- 1/2 tsp sugar
- 1/2 tsp cracked black pepper
- 1/2 tsp salt
- 25ml olive oil
- 25g butter
- Rocket

Red wine reduction:
- 1/2 cup red wine
- 1/2 cup chicken stock
- 1/2 tsp caster sugar
- 1 tablespoon butter

Method:
1. Brush shank with olive oil, season with salt and pepper and then coat with crushed garlic.
2. In a casserole dish that can be used on the stovetop, seal the shank well in the remaining oil and butter on a baking tray. Bake for about 10 minutes.
3. Chop onion, tomatoes, capsicum and bacon. Saute with shank.
4. Add in bayleaf, tomato paste, red wine, water and put lid on pan and place in a fan forced oven at 150°C for 3 hours, stirring every half hour, topping up with water if necessary so that it doesn't dry out.
5. Take lamb out and rest.
6. Slice lamb and place back in casserole dish.
7. Put the dish back on the stovetop and reduce the mixture if necessary.
8. Use the outline of a small 10cm square tin to cut pastry.
9. Place the pastry in a muffin tray. Spoon mixture into the middle of the pastry and crumble fetta on top.
10. Place back in a fan forced oven at 200°C for 10 minutes. Then take out of muffin tray and place on flat tray for a further 5 minutes to ensure the bottom of the pastry is cooked.
11. While the tart is in the oven, make the red wine reduction by boiling the wine, chicken stock and sugar, and reducing the liquid by about half.
12. Reduce to simmer and whisk in 1 tablespoon butter.
13. Serve tart on top of rocket, with red wine reduction drizzled around tart.

Drink with this...

Shiraz

"Full bodied and very smooth. It's brimming with juicy black and red berry fruit flavours with a hint of warm spice and vanilla... a wine perfect for full flavoured dishes."

Bow tie pasta with amoroso tomato

Ingredients:
2 large bacon rashers
2 small onions
1 large garlic clove
100g pine nuts
10 vine ripened amoroso tomatoes
60g Romano cheese
1/2 cup chopped baby spinach
150-200g bow tie pasta
4 tbs olive oil
*Can be served with a side of salad

Method:
1. Chop bacon into small pieces and finely chop onion.
2. Turn fan forced oven to 160°C and place in two pairs of amoroso tomatoes on a baking tray. Bake for about 10 minutes.
3. Follow the directions to cook the bow tie pasta in boiling water.
4. Saute onion and bacon, turn up heat to achieve some caramelisation.
5. Turn the heat back down and add pine nuts and garlic.
6. Quarter the remaining amoroso tomatoes and gently stir through, with chopped spinach.
7. Crumble about 50g of Romano cheese into mixture and stir through.
8. Drain pasta and add to pan with bacon and tomato mixture, and gently stir through.
9. Serve with roasted tomatoes and shavings of Romano cheese.

Drink with this...

Shiraz Sangiovese Rose

"A judicious blend of Shiraz and Sangiovese. Fresh berry and apple fruit flavours balanced by crisp acidity."

Melted heart chocolate pudding

Ingredients:
1/3 cup plain flour
1 tbs SR flour
2 tbs icing sugar
180g dark chocolate melted
50g butter melted
1/2 tsp vanilla essence
1 egg
2 egg yolks

chocolate sauce:
1/2 cup melted chocolate
1/4 cup cream

pudding sauce:
30ml Tia Maria
*Can be served with cream or ice-cream.

Method:
1. Set fan forced oven to 140°C.
2. Get two ramekins, for this recipe, mine are circular, 6cm in width at the top, and 6cm in height, and 4cm in width at the base.
3. Generously grease with butter and then coat with sugar.
4. Mix together all ingredients for pudding.
5. Fill ramekin 3/4 full with pudding mixture.
6. Pour Tia Maria over the top of the pudding mixture so that it covers the mixture to a depth of 2mm.
7. Place in oven for 20 minutes.
8. Melt chocolate for sauce, in heatproof bowl over simmering water. Stir through cream.
9. Take ramekins out of oven and sit for 1 minute. Use a knife to loosen the edges of the pudding to make it easy to turn out.
10. Pour hot sauce over the top of turned out pudding, and serve straight away.

Drink with this...

Sparling Shiraz

"With aromas of dark plums followed by a velvet blast of soft, juicy black fruits with a hint of dark chocolate. It's a great aperitif and a flying start to any celebration. Best with roast turkey or duck, or with dessert."

Zucchini cakes & flower salad

Ingredients:
2 zucchini flowers
1 cup grated zucchini
1 cup grated potato
1/4 cup grated carrot
1 egg
1/4 cup plain flour
1/2 tsp bicarbonate soda
1/2 tsp chilli powder
1/2 tsp crushed garlic
salt and pepper
1/4 cup olive oil

salad:
rocket
2 shallots
1/4 red capsicum
1/4 yellow capsicum

dressing:
1/4 cup apple cider vinegar
1 tbs lemon
2 tbs boiling water
1 tsp sugar

Method:
1. Carefully open the zucchini flowers and remove stamen.
2. Cut capsicum and shallots into thin strips and mix with rocket, and set aside.
3. For dressing: Dissolve sugar in boiling water, then add lemon juice, apple cider vinegar and place in a small jug. Place in fridge.
4. Mix together oil, chilli and garlic, for shallow frying zucchini cakes.
5. Grate carrot, zucchini and potato and mix with egg, flour and bicarbonate soda. Season with salt and pepper.
6. Mould into little cakes and dust with flour.
7. Shallow fry in oil mix.
8. Take out of pan and pat dry with paper towel.
9. Mix together rocket, shallots, capsicum in a bowl and toss with dressing.
10. Serve zucchini cakes with zucchini flower on top and salad inside flower.
11. Drizzle balsamic vinegar on plate to serve.

Drink with this...

Pinot Grigio

"The palate is full, comprising a richness akin to the variety. With a clean lime and grapefruit crispness, it is complemented by the tropical fruit nuances. Best with salad and seafood."

Duck a la rose

Ingredients:
2 duck breasts
2 potatoes
6 baby carrots
1 tablespoon butter
1 cup red wine
1 cup chicken stock
1 tbs red wine vinegar
1 red rose
1 tbs brown sugar
1 tsp arrowroot
salt
pepper

Method:
1. Score the skin of the duck breast and season with salt.
2. Place a tablespoon of butter in a hot frying pan and place duck breast with skin side down and cook until brown. Turn and seal underside of duck.
3. Place in a fan forced oven at 200°C for 5 minutes and then reduce heat to 175°C for a further 10 minutes. Remove from oven and rest meat on a cutting board for 30 minutes.
4. Combine wine, stock, vinegar, rose petals, sugar, salt and pepper in a blender and blend for 5 minutes, then strain into a small pot. Bring to boil and reduce by half, then take off heat.
5. Peel potatoes and make 8 parallel incisions in each, making sure not to slice all the way through. Brush with olive oil and place in oven, continually basting at 200°C for around 30 minutes or until cooked.
6. Steam carrots.
7. Return duck to oven for 10 minutes or until heated through.
8. Reheat sauce and combine 1 tsp arrowroot with 2 tbs water and mix together and then add to sauce combining well. Bring to the boil, to thicken the sauce and then take off heat.
9. Slice duck and serve with sauce, carrot and potato.

Drink with this...

Shiraz Malbec

"This is a great blend of the best Shiraz and Malbec. The Shiraz gives plenty of body and peppery spice, whilst the Malbec gives the wine its ripe fruit flavours and rich colour. Perfect for pasta, duck and BBQs."

Rosewater & white chocolate mousse

Ingredients:
90g melted white chocolate
1/2 cup cream
2 eggs separated
3 tbs icing sugar
1/4 tsp rosewater
1 tbs gelatine
1/4 cup water

Raspberry centre:
1/2 cup raspberries
1 tbs caster sugar
1 tbs boiling water

Crumble:
2 Anzac biscuits crushed

Method:
1. In a double saucepan over simmering water, melt chocolate and add egg yolks, beating until thick.
2. In another double saucepan over simmering water, combine gelatine and water and stir until fully dissolved and reduced by half.
3. Add gelatine mix with rosewater, and then slowly add to chocolate, combining well.
4. Whip cream and add icing sugar, making sure it is well combined. Be careful not to overwhip.
5. Fold cream into chocolate mixture.
6. In a clean bowl, beat egg whites until they form soft white peaks.
7. Fold egg whites in small portions, into chocolate and cream mix.
8. To make raspberry centre, dissolve caster sugar in boiling water, and blend together with raspberries. Strain through a fine tea strainer.
10. Pour half the mousse in each glass, followed by a layer of raspberry, and then top with the remaining mousse.
11. Crumble biscuit on top to serve.

Drink with this...

Sparkling Moscato

"Take the time to sprite your senses with an apricot tingle sensation. If that isn't sufficient combine some honeysuckle. A great combination to all celebrations and moments worth remembering."

Winter menu

June
E: Hommus sweet hommus
M: Hearty pie
D: Sweetie pie

July
E: Soup of pomme d'amour
M: Moussaka with pomme d'amour
D: Lovers' chocolate fondue for two

August
E: Crouton heart with poached egg, hollandaise and bacon ribbons
M: Beef cutlet with red rose & wine jus
D: Chantilly kisses for a king

Hommus sweet hommus

Ingredients:
200g chick peas
1 clove garlic crushed
5 tsp white vinegar
2 tbs lemon juice
1 tsp white pepper
3 tbs tahini paste
120ml water
180ml olive oil
2 tsp cumin
1 1/2 tsp salt
1 tsp paprika
2 tortillas
150g diced lamb

marinade:
2 tbs oil
2 tsp garlic
2 tsp cumin
1 tsp paprika

Method:
1. Soak chick peas in water for 6 hours. Drain, then place in a large pot and fill with 5 litres of fresh water and bring to the boil. Reduce heat and simmer for 45 minutes, then drain.
2. Combine all ingredients for hommus (except for marinade, tortillas and lamb) and place in a blender. Process well until thick and creamy. Cover and refrigerate.
3. Combine marinade and coat over diced lamb and place on a skewer.
4. Cut a small circle out of the tortilla and place in a small bowl, then bake in a fan forced oven at 180°C for 5 minutes.
5. Place a tablespoon of oil in a hot pan and lightly pan-fry the marinated lamb.
6. Serve hommus in tortilla, with lamb on side.

Drink with this...
Malbec

"Positioned between robust and soft, this succulent wine is fruity with spice. The aroma has a hint of plums, cherries and raspberries. Serve with BBQ and Mediterranean cuisine."

Hearty pie

Ingredients:
1 tbs oil
1 small onion finely chopped
2 small tomatoes diced
500g porterhouse steak diced
1 clove garlic crushed
2 cups beef stock
2 tablespoons tomato paste
1/2 tsp thyme
pinch nutmeg
2 tbs plain flour
1/2 cup water
salt and pepper
2 sheets puff pastry
1 egg (for eggwash)
2tbs milk (for eggwash)

Mash:
4 medium potatoes
20g butter
50ml milk
salt
pinch nutmeg
*Can be served with a side of salad or vegetables

Method:
1. Saute onion in a pan and brown beef.
2. Combine all ingredients for pie filling and place in a thick ceramic bowl. Place in a fan forced oven at 180°C, with the lid on, for 1 1/2 hours, stirring every half hour.
3. Once pie filling is cooked, make mash by steaming the potatoes until soft and then mashing together with other ingredients.
4. Use a deep single serve dish to cut a mould for the pastry lid of the pie.
5. Spoon filling into two deep single serve dishes. Fill to just under the edge of the bowls, then top with potato mash.
6. Top with pastry, pressing firmly into sides of dish. Use a cookie cutter to cut the shape of a heart.
7. In a small bowl, mix egg and milk to make eggwash. Baste pastry with eggwash and place heart in centre on top of pie and baste with eggwash again.
8. Bake in a fan forced oven at 180°C for 5-10 minutes or until golden.

Drink with this...
Cabernet Sauvignon

"This classic Cabernet has deep purple colour, boasting aromas of blackcurrant, dark chocolate and vanilla with subtle earthy characters."

Sweetie pie

Ingredients:
1/2 cup champagne
1/3 cup sugar
1/2 tsp cinnamon
60g butter
1/2 tsp lemon juice
6 wild hibiscus flowers
2 tbs water
1 tbs corn flour
1/4 cup wild hibiscus syrup
1.5 kilos of green apples

Pastry:
1/4 cup caster sugar
1 3/4 cup plain flour
3/4 cup SR flour
1 egg
180 g butter
*Can be served with cream or icecream

Method:
1. Peel, core and quarter apples, then cut into eighths.
2. Blend together water, hibiscus flowers and hibiscus syrup.
3. Combine this syrup with champagne, sugar, cinnamon, lemon and bring to boil. Reduce heat, adding apples to simmer for one hour and add 60g butter.
5. Combine 1/4 cup water with corn flour and pour into the apple mixture, mix well to avoid any lumps. Bring to boil again then take off heat.
6. To make pastry, use a large mxing bowl and combine flour, sugar and softened butter and mix together until it resembles fine breadcrumbs.
7. Add egg and then divide mixture into one portion of 2/5 and the other portion 3/5.
8. Refrigerate for one hour. Grease dish.
9. Roll pastry in between two sheets of baking paper, using the larger portion to line the dish with a thickness of about 1/2 cm.
10. Spoon in filling.
11. Cut the remaining pastry into long strips and working from the centre, arrange pastry vertically and then horizontally and so on until covered.
12. Bake at 180°C in a fan forced oven for 20 minutes, then at 160°C for a further 20 minutes.

Drink with this...

Peace in my soul

"A little sweet and a little bubbly, just like you! Live with Peace in your soul, and share the enlightenment... and the wine... with your friends. Isn't that what it's all about?"

Soup of pomme d'amour

Ingredients:
- 1 tbs oil
- 2 small onions chopped
- 1 large clove garlic crushed
- 1 tsp rosewater
- 3 bacon rashers chopped
- 1 tsp chilli powder
- 1/2 tsp vanilla essence
- 1 tsp sugar
- pinch of cinnamon
- 24 icecubes
- 1 kilo roma tomatoes
- 3 tbs tomato paste
- 1 1/2 cups chicken stock
- 2 litres of water
- 150ml red wine
- 2 tbs chopped chives
- 1 tsp thyme
- salt
- cracked black pepper
- Pecorino cheese
- 2 slices of bread
- Basil to garnish

Method:
1. In a large pan, boil water, then simmer.
2. Have a large bowl full of cold water and icecubes ready.
3. Place half the tomatoes in the simmering water, making sure they are fully submerged for about 1-2 minutes. Then transfer straight to cold water.
4. Do the same with the remaining tomatoes.
5. Score the bottom of the tomato and the skin will easily peel away.
6. Discard skin and chop tomatoes.
7. Heat oil in large pot. Fry onions and bacon.
8. Add all other ingredients and bring to the boil, then reduce to a simmer for 60 minutes. Top up with water if the soup reduces too much in consistency.
9. Blend with hand held blender and reduce to simmer.
10. Cut heart shapes from bread and lightly brush with olive oil and then place in a fan forced oven at 180ºC for 5 minutes or until light brown. Grate some Pecorino cheese on top and then place in the middle of a bowl filled with soup. Grill to make the cheese golden in colour. Serve with a garnish of fresh basil.

Drink with this...
Shiraz

"Full bodied and very smooth. It's brimming with juicy black and red berry fruit flavours with a hint of warm spice and vanilla... a wine perfect for full flavoured dishes."

Moussaka with pomme d'amour

Ingredients:
250g mince lamb
20g butter
1 small onion
1 clove garlic crushed
1/4 cup shiraz
1 cup water
1/4 cup currants
3 cups soup of pomme d'amour
pinch nutmeg
2 Lebanese eggplants
2 zucchini
2 potatoes
salt
2 tbs oil

bechamel:
1 dried bay leaf
25g butter
2 tbs plain flour
1 cup milk
pinch nutmeg
salt
white pepper

*Can be served with a side of salad or vegetables

Method:
1. Finely slice eggplant into long strips. Slice potato. Slice zucchini into long strips and then halve to make long thin strips.
2. Heat 2 tbs oil in a pan.
3. Gently saute potato, eggplant and zucchini. Set aside.
4. Heat butter and add meat, onion and garlic. Cook until onions become transluscent. Add garlic, soup, wine, currants, water and nutmeg together and bring to the boil, then reduce to simmer.
5. Reduce mixture to a thick consistency, but still leave plenty of moisture.
6. Make bechamel sauce: heat butter, add flour and then add milk slowly. Bring to boil, thicken and season with salt and pepper. Add nutmeg.
7. Get a coffee cup and brush with olive oil. Layer eggplant and zucchini around the cup, and then use a thick layer of zucchini around the top of the cup.
8. Press a layer of potato around the edges to help hold in the mixture.
9. Put two tablespoons of bechamel in the bottom, and then fill with mince mixture and top with potato. Bake in a fan forced oven at 180°c for 25 minutes.
10. Stand for 5 minutes, then turn out of cup and garnish with tomato and shallot.

Drink with this...
Shiraz Sangiovese Rose

"A judicious blend of Shiraz and Sangiovese. Fresh berry and apple fruit flavours balanced by crisp acidity."

Lovers' chocolate fondue for two

Ingredients:
50ml thinkened cream
30ml Tia Maria
100g dark chocolate
8 strawberries
8 chocolate sticks
2 pieces of chocolate slice halved

raspberry jam

Method:
1. Heat cream and then stir in Tia Maria.
2. Place chocolate in a heatproof bowl over simmering water and pour cream over chocolate until all melted.
3. Place strawberries on end of chocolate sticks by making a small hole for the sticks to be inserted.
4. Cut chocolate slice in half.
5. Make a little decoration with raspberry jam in a sauce bottle by zig zagging.
6. Place slice on top of jam, with strawberries on sticks and chocolate sauce in a small serving bowl and serve.

Drink with this...

Sparling Shiraz

"With aromas of dark plums followed by a velvet blast of soft, juicy black fruits with a hint of dark chocolate. It's a great aperitif and a flying start to any celebration. Best with roast turkey or duck, or with dessert."

Crouton heart with poached egg

Ingredients:
4 rashers bacon
1 uncut loaf of bread
6 eggs
cracked black pepper
1 1/2 tbs lemon juice
200g salted butter
1/2 tbs white vinegar
olive oil

Method:
hollandaise
1. Chop butter into small cubes and stand until it becomes softened.
2. In a double saucepan, bring water to boil, then reduce to simmer and place heatproof bowl on top.
3. Whisk 4 egg yolks until light in colour and slowly add butter, piece by piece until all combined. Don't let the mixture boil or get too hot.
4. Whisk in lemon juice slowly, then vinegar and add pepper.

crouton and curled bacon ribbons
1. Use a heart shaped cookie cutter or mould to cut a small heart shaped crouton, about 2 cm in depth.
2. Brush with olive oil.
3. Cut bacon into long thin strips and curl around a thick metal rod, or some aluminium foil rolled up to imitate a rod.
4. Place bacon in oven for 15 minutes and crouton for last 10 minutes at a temperature of 200°C in a fan forced oven.

poached egg
1. Crack an egg into a small and shallow dish.
2. Stir simmering water, that has a depth of about 3 inches, in a small shallow pot in clockwise direction.
3. Carefully lower egg into centre of water, and cook for 1-2 minutes. Serve on top of crouton, with bacon on the side and hollandaise sauce on top.

Drink with this...
Chardonnay

"*A lovely crisp wine, elegant and bristling with tropical fruit flavours. Not heavily oaked so it's great for drinking chilled, on its own. It's also worth trying with fresh fish and grilled chicken salads.*"

Beef cutlet with red rose & wine jus

Ingredients:
2 beef fillets on the bone
6 tbs olive oil
1 small red chilli chopped
1 tsp crushed garlic
2 cups red wine

mash:
3 tbs butter
3 large potatoes
450ml thickened cream
salt to taste

jus:
2 cups beef stock
2 cups red wine
1/2 tsp crushed garlic
2 red roses
2 tsp butter
*Can be served with a side of salad or vegetables

Method:
1. Brush fillets with oil, garlic and chilli.
2. Place in deep tray and pour over wine and sit for 2 hours.
3. Take out of tray and seal beef in very hot pan and then place in a fan forced oven at 180ºC for 10 minutes.
4. Take out of oven and rest meat for one hour in pan.
5. To make jus, blend stock, garlic and rose petals. Strain through tea towel.
6. Peel potatoes and cook until soft.
7. Take meat out of pan and place on chopping board.
8. Heat the pan that was used to cook the meat, and add wine, bringing to the boil to cook off the alcohol. Add stock and reduce jus a little then take off heat.
9. Place beef in a fan forced oven at 200ºC for 10 minutes.
10. Combine all ingredients for mash.
11. Just before being ready to serve, put jus on low heat to warm up and then take off heat and add butter to get a silky smooth consistency.
12. Place cutlet on a bed of mash and pour jus around.

Drink with this...

Shiraz

"*Full bodied and very smooth. It's brimming with juicy black and red berry fruit flavours with a hint of warm spice and vanilla... a wine perfect for full flavoured dishes.*"

Chantilly kisses for a king

Ingredients:
60g butter (room temperature)
1/4 cup brown sugar
1 egg
1/2 tsp vanilla essence
1 tsp cinnamon
3/4 cup plain flour
1 tbs SR flour
90g melted white chocolate
1/2 cup milk

chantilly cream:
1 cup thickened cream
3 tbs icing sugar
1 tsp vanilla essence
2 wild hibiscus flowers
wild hibiscus syrup

Method:
1. Cream butter and sugar together.
2. Add all other ingredients and make sure they are well combined.
3. Grease and line a small tin (10cm square) with baking paper.
4. Bake in a fan forced oven at 140°C for 35 minutes or until a skewer comes out clean.
5. Place on rack to cool.
6. Beat cream, adding vanilla and sugar.
7. Slice the cake with a sharp knife, and then use a cookie cutter to make flower shapes.
8. Layer cake and cream, and serve with wild hibiscus flower and syrup.

Drink with this...
Sparkling Moscato

"Take the time to sprite your senses with an apricot tingle sensation. If that isn't sufficient combine some honeysuckle. A great combination to all celebrations and moments worth remembering."

Spring menu

September
E: Zucchini flowers with bacon & fetta
M: Chilli lovers' chicken
D: Sweet heart cheese cake

October
E: Lovers' heart terrine
M: Honeyglazed spatchcock
D: French kissed raspberries

November
E: Avocado & a roma tomato with champagne vinaigrette
M: Heart & soul cakes
D: Tia Maria & dark chocolate icecream

Zucchini flowers with bacon & fetta

Ingredients:
6 zucchini flowers
1 cup plain flour
1 egg
1 cup soda water cold
24 ice cubes
2 small zucchinis
2 rashers of bacon
1/2 tsp crushed garlic
1/2 small onion
1 tsp thyme
90g fetta
1/4 cup chopped baby spinach
1/2 tsp cracked black pepper

Method:
1. Gently open zucchini flowers and remove stamen, making sure not to tear the flower. Give them a gentle rinse in water.
2. Finely chop onion and bacon, and saute in pan.
3. Chop spinach, and place in mixing bowl with thyme, pepper and grated fetta.
4. Add sauted onion and bacon, and garlic.
5. Mix well with fork.
6. Slice zucchinis and lightly pan fry.
7. Open zucchini flowers, being careful not to tear the flower, and spoon in mixture, filling the flower just over half way.
8. Twist the ends of the flower, dust in plain flour.
9. Mix together flour, egg, and soda water until the mixture has a smooth consistency. Add icecubes.
10. Heat oil for frying.
11. Dip flowers through mixture, making sure to coat the entire flower and gently lower into oil, cooking until golden.

Drink with this...
Sauvignon Blanc

"This wine exhibits a fragrant nose of snow peas with a little passionfruit, coupled with a clean citrus and crisp acidity. Great fruit length and generous fruit driven flavours."

Chilli lovers' chicken

Ingredients:
2 cups champagne
3 small red chillies
2 tsp crushed garlic
1 tbs lemon juice
2 tbs olive oil
2 chicken breasts

stuffed tomato:
1/2 tsp onion powder
2 trussed tomatoes
5 tbs water
1 tbs oil
1/2 tsp chilli powder
1 tsp chives
1/2 red onion
1/2 cup cous cous
1/3 cup chicken stock
*Can be served with a side of salad or vegetables

Method:
1. Saute chopped onions and then mix with water, oil, chilli powder, chopped chives, onion powder, chicken stock and cous cous.
2. Stand for one hour.
3. Take two chicken breasts and marinate in champagne, chopped chillies, garlic, lemon and oil for 1 hour.
4. Slice top off tomato, hollow out and fill with cous cous.
5. Place in oven for a total of half an hour.
6. Take out chicken and pan fry for 5 minutes each side and then place in a fan forced oven at 180°C for a further 10-15 minutes or until cooked.
7. Serve with a lettuce garnish.

Drink with this...

Chardonnay

"A lovely crisp wine, elegant and bristling with tropical fruit flavours. Not heavily oaked so it's great for drinking chilled, on its own. It's also worth trying with fresh fish and grilled chicken salads."

Sweet heart cheese cake

Ingredients:
base:
150g Scotch finger biscuits
150g Marie biscuits
150g butter
40g finely chopped macadamia nuts
40g finely chopped white chocolate
1 tsp cinnamon sugar

filling:
180g melted white chocolate
500g cream cheese
2 tsp vanilla essence
3 eggs
1/2 cup caster sugar
1 tbs rosewater

Method:
1. Crush biscuits, combine cinnamon, melted butter, chopped chocolate and nuts.
2. Press over base and sides of 8 inch springform pan.
3. Refrigerate.
4. Beat cream cheese until soft.
5. In a clean bowl, beat eggs until they become thick and then slowly add sugar. Keep beating and slowly add cream cheese.
6. Add vanilla and melted chocolate as well as rosewater and combine all ingredients until smooth.
7. Spread into the crust and bake at 175°C in a fan forced oven for 20 minutes.
8. Cool and then refrigerate, for best results, for 24 hours.
9. To serve, garnish with wild hibiscus flower and syrup.

Drink with this...
Riesling

"Enjoy at the end of a meal or any occasion. A light bodied, refreshing and easy drinking sweet wine with a hint of pear and a clean crisp finish."

Lovers' heart terrine

Ingredients:
1 large kipfler potato
50g marinated red pepper
200g sliced prosciutto
2 cups cous cous
1 egg
1 tsp garlic
1/2 tsp chilli powder
2 cups chicken stock
1/2 cup water
2 tbs olive oil
oil for frying

Method:
1. Mix together egg, garlic, chilli, stock, water and oil
2. Pour in cous cous, making sure it is covered by liquid. Stand for 1 hour.
3. Peel and cut potato to a long heart shape to fit easily into a 10cm square terrine tin.
4. Deep fry potato heart chip, ensuring fully cooked.
5. Line terrine dish with baking paper.
6. Line dish with prosciutto, leaving enough out to cover the top once the terrine dish is filled.
7. Fill 1/2 dish with cous cous.
8. Wrap chip in red pepper, and place in the middle of the terrine.
9. Fill rest of terrine with cous cous and wrap top with prosciutto.
10. Place in a fan forced oven at 180°C for 40 minutes.
11. Remove from oven. Allow to stand until cool, then take out of terrine dish.
12. Cool in refrigerator, then slice and serve with salad garnish.

*Note which way potato heart is facing, so that when you slice terrine, heart shape will appear in the middle.

Drink with this...

Pinot Grigio

"The palate is full, comprising a richness akin to the variety. With a clean lime and grapefruit crispness, it is complemented by the tropical fruit nuances. Best with salad and seafood."

Honeyglazed spatchcock

Ingredients:
1 spatchcock
12 baby potatoes

Honey glaze:
125g honey
30ml soy
1/4 cup champagne or sparkling wine

stuffing:
1 small chopped onion
1 rasher bacon
1 tsp rosemary, sage, thyme
1 egg
1/2 cup breadcrumbs
1/2 cup chicken stock
1 tsp crushed garlic
salt
pepper
*Can be served with a side of salad or vegetables

Method:
1. Finely chop onion and bacon and saute.
2. In a mixing bowl, combine all ingredients for stuffing.
3. Put stuffing in spatchcock and use cooking twine to bind legs together, and if necessary, toothpicks to keep wings in place.
4. Combine mixture for honeyglaze and baste spatchcock.
5. Place in a fan forced oven at 175°C for half an hour, basting every 10 minutes.
6. Take out of oven and rest for one hour and continue to baste.
7. Return to oven for 20 minutes, serve with roasted potatoes.

Drink with this...
Shiraz Malbec

"This is a great blend of the best Shiraz and Malbec. The Shiraz gives plenty of body and peppery spice, whilst the Malbec gives the wine its ripe fruit flavours and rich colour. Perfect for pasta, duck and BBQs."

French kissed raspberries

Ingredients:
filo pastry
2 punnets raspberries
400ml thickened cream
40g dark chocolate
1/2 cup champagne
1 tbs icing sugar
1/2 tsp vanilla essence
1/2 tsp rosewater

Method:
1. Marinate raspberries in champagne and rosewater for half an hour.
2. Whip cream with vanilla essence and icing sugar.
3. Carefully separate sheets of filo pastry and place in oven at 180°C for 1-2 minutes.
4. Cut into 5cm squares and set aside (make 20 squares in total).
5. Melt chocolate in heatproof dish over simmering water.
6. Pair off the squares and place chocolate in the middle of each pair and press together.
7. Drain raspberries and pat dry.
8. Layer squares, cream, raspberries.
9. Stack raspberries on top and dust with icing sugar to serve.

Drink with this...

Sparkling Moscato

"Take the time to sprite your senses with an apricot tingle sensation. If that isn't sufficient combine some honeysuckle. A great combination to all celebrations and moments worth remembering."

Avocado & a roma tomato with champagne vinaigrette

Ingredients:
1 avocado
4 roma tomatoes

viniagrette:
2 tbs honey
2 tbs champagne
2 tbs white wine vinegar
1 tbs vegetable oil
1 tsp dijon mustard
cracked black pepper

Method:
1. Mix together honey, champagne, vinegar, mustard and pepper with a whisk.
2. Halve avocado, take out the seed and slice lengthways.
3. Take the roma tomato, and using a sharp knife start from the bottom and peel the skin just as you would an apple, in one long fine strip.
4. Roll the tomato skin up to form a rose.
5. Slice the other roma tomato and fan out the avocado and tomato and drizzle with viniagrette.

Drink with this...

Sauvignon Blanc

"This wine exhibits a fragrant nose of snow peas with a little passionfruit, coupled with a clean citrus and crisp acidity. Great fruit length and generous fruit driven flavours."

Heart & soul cakes

Ingredients:
250g potatoes
20g butter
1/2 small onion
1/2 celery stick
250g sole or mild flavoured fish
plain flour for dusting
1 cup bread crumbs
fresh chives for presentation

dipping sauce:
118ml champagne or sparkling wine
1 tsp dijon mustard
1 tsp lemon juice
2 egg yolks
125g cubed butter
salt and white pepper
*Can be served with a side of salad or vegetables

Method:
1. Steam potatoes and mash with 20g butter.
2. Finely chop onion, celery, fish and mix in with potatoes.
3. Add garlic, chilli, chives, dill, lemon and season with salt and pepper.
4. Mould into croquettes, dust with flour, dip in egg and roll in breadcrumbs.
5. Shallow fry until golden, place in oven to remain warm.

dipping sauce:
1. Prepare dipping sauce by placing a heatproof bowl over simmering water and place champagne in bowl, reduce by about half and then set aside to cool a little.
2. Place heatproof bowl with champagne back over simmering water. Add 2 egg yolks and whisk until paler in colour and liquid becomes very warm. Be careful not to boil liquid.
3. Add mustard and lemon juice and whisk in. Add salt and pepper.
4. Add the softened cubed butter, whisking it in, one cube at a time. Mixture should thicken, then take off heat. Serve the fish with chives and dipping sauce.

Drink with this...
Chardonnay

"A lovely crisp wine, elegant and bristling with tropical fruit flavours. Not heavily oaked so it's great for drinking chilled, on its own. It's also worth trying with fresh fish and grilled chicken salads."

Dark chocolate & Tia Maria ice-cream

Ingredients:
400ml cream
4 egg yolks
1/2 cup caster sugar
30ml Tia Maria
1/2 tsp vanilla essence
50g grated dark chocolate

Method:
1. Using a hand held beater, beat cream, egg and vanilla, then place in heatproof bowl over simmering water.
2. Continue beating, adding sugar in small parts until mixture thickens and becomes light in colour (making sure not to let the mixture come to the boil).
3. Take off heat and use hand held beaters to beat for a further 5 minutes, stirring in Tia Maria and grated chocolate.
4. Use mixmaster to beat for 5-10 minutes until light and fluffy.
5. Freeze for 1 1/2 hours and then rebeat, until mixture becomes pale in colour.
6. Place back in freezer. For best results, freeze for 24 hours.

Drink with this...

Peace in my soul White

"A little sweet and a little bubbly, just like you! Live with Peace in your soul, and share the enlightenment... and the wine... with your friends. Isn't that what it's all about?"

Special occasion menu

Every day is a special occasion. It's just that some days are extra special – and therefore need to be especially celebrated

Special occasion menu...

A great apertif!

Serve in a little glass before the meal. It helps to make the occasion a little more special and will help to stimulate the appetite for the meal that is to follow. It is a "little sweet and a little bubbly — just like you! Live with Peace in your heart, and Peace in your soul, and share the love...and the wine... with your friends.
Isn't that what it's all about?"

with Peace in my heart & Peace in my soul.

Special date:
- E: Lamb rosettes with date paste
- M: Date with Moroccan lamb
- D: Date pudding

Valentine's Day
- E: Cupid's arrow of sugar & spice beef
- M: Lamb shank in cannelloni with roasted love apple
- D: Red velvet cake

Wedding anniversary
- E: Rings of butterfly pork
- M: Lamb married with sweet pepper
- D: White wedding cake

Lamb rosettes with date paste

Ingredients:
300g lamb leg steaks
4 tablespoons marinated capsicum cut into thin strips
2 tablespoons olive oil
1 date
1 tsp rosemary
1 tsp crushed garlic
1 tsp tomato paste
1 tsp chopped chives
2 cherry tomatoes
2 wedges of double brie

Method:
1. Mix together capsicum, oil, date, garlic, tomato paste, rosemary and chives and mash with fork to form a paste.
2. Cut steak into long, thin strips, and then coat with paste.
3. Roll up and place on skewer and coat outside.
4. Place 1 tbs oil in a hot pan and brown each side, then place in a fan forced oven at 220°C for 10 minutes.
5. Serve with a wedge of double brie and a cherry tomato

Drink with this...
Cabernet Sauvignon Merlot

"This is a really powerful, full bodied red with plenty of delicious blackberry and ripe plum flavours. A serious yet smooth mouthful, which is perfect with full savoury dishes and cheese."

Date with Moroccan lamb

Ingredients:
400g diced lamb

spice mix for lamb:
1/2 tsp of:
nutmeg
coriander
ginger
white pepper
chilli powder
paprika
turmeric
cinnamon
ground black pepper
salt
1 tsp cumin

stew:
2 cups vegetable stock
2 litres water
1 onion
1 red chilli
1 carrot
1 celery stick
2 tomatoes
2 potatoes
2 cloves garlic crushed
2 tbs oil
60g pitted dates
1/2 cup chopped flat leaf parsley

to serve:
2 round bread rolls
chives to garnish
1 1/2 tbs arrowroot

Method:
1. Chop all ingredients for stew, and combine with stock and water in a casserole dish with lid on and then place in a fan forced oven at 160°C for 2 hours.
2. Hollow out bread roll and brush with oil and set aside.
3. Dice lamb and coat lamb with spice mix, cover and refrigerate for 2 hours.
4. In a hot pan, seal meat and add to casserole dish, cooking in oven for another 2 hours at 160°C in a fan forced oven.
5. Remove from oven and cook on medium heat with lid on stovetop for about an hour. Add more water if necessary.
6. After an hour, start to reduce on low heat on stovetop.
7. When mixture has reduced enough, mix 1 1/2 tbs arrowroot in 3 tbs water and slowly mix into casserole, allowing to thicken.
8. Place bread rolls in oven for 5-10 minutes or until crusty.
9. Spoon casserole into bread rolls and garnish with chives.

Drink with this...
Malbec

"Positioned between robust and soft, this succulent wine is fruity with spice. The aroma has a hint of plums, cherries and raspberries. Serve with BBQ and Mediterranean cuisine."

Date pudding

Ingredients:
1/3 cup plain flour
1 tbs SR flour
2 tbs icing sugar
180g white chocolate melted
50g butter melted
1/2 tsp vanilla essence
1 egg
2 egg yolks
80g dates pitted and chopped

sauce:
1/2 cup brown sugar
200ml thickened cream
1/2 tsp vanilla essence
40g butter
*Can be served with cream and/or ice-cream.

Method:
1. Set fan forced oven to 140°C.
2. Get two ramekins, for this recipe, mine are circular, 6cm in width at the top and in height, and 4cm at the base.
3. Generously grease with butter and then coat with sugar.
4. Mix together all ingredients for pudding.
5. Fill ramekin 3/4 full with pudding mixture.
6. Place in oven for 20 minutes.
7. Melt butter for sauce.
8. Combine all ingredients for sauce in a small saucepan and bring to the boil. Reduce the mixture by about half, until it is a thick consistency.
9. Take ramekins out of oven and sit for 1 minute. Use a knife to loosen the edges of the pudding to make it easy to turn out.
10. Pour hot sauce over the top of turned out pudding and serve straight away.

Drink with this...

Peace in my heart red

"A little sweet and a little bubbly, just like you! Live with Peace in your heart, and share the love... and the wine... with your friends. Isn't that what it's all about?"

Cupid's arrow of sugar & spice beef

Ingredients:
- 1 punnet large cherry tomatoes
- 1 large red onion
- 2 small zucchinis
- 1 punnet button mushrooms
- 500g rump steak cubed
- 1 cup rice

marinade:
- 2tbs corn flour
- 1 1/4 cups water
- 1/4 cup red wine
- 1/4 cup red wine vinegar
- 1/2 tsp onion powder
- 1/2 tsp garlic powder
- 1/4 tsp chilli powder
- 1/4 cup sugar
- 1/3 cup soy

Method:
1. Mix sugar and water together and heat in a pan on stovetop until sugar has dissolved.
2. Add red wine and bring to boil to cook off alcohol.
3. In a cup mix wheaten flour with 1/4 cup of water to form a paste and add to the mixture in the saucepan, whisking so that lumps do not appear and bring to the boil again.
4. Once mixture has thickened, take off heat and add remaining ingredients for marinade and whisk to achieve a thick and smooth consistency. Cool.
5. Arrange steak, tomatoes, onion, zucchini and mushrooms on a skewer and place in an airtight container, with the marinade poured over the top of the skewers, then refrigerate overnight for best results.
6. Cook on stovetop in a saucepan, or grill on the BBQ.

Drink with this...

Cabernet Sauvignon Merlot

"This is a really powerful, full bodied red with plenty of delicious blackberry and ripe plum flavours. A serious yet smooth mouthful, which is perfect with full savoury dishes and cheese."

Lamb shank in cannelloni with roasted love apple

Ingredients:
2 lamb shanks
1 tsp garlic
2 litres of water
1/4 cup red wine
4 whole tomatoes
1/2 cup chopped parsley
1 bacon rasher
1 tbs wheaten flour
parsley

1 onion chopped
1 bayleaf
1 tsp thyme
2 tablespoons tomato paste
50g butter
fresh lasagne sheets
olive oil
salt and pepper

*Can be served with a side of salad or vegetables

Method:
1. Melt butter and add garlic, shanks, onion and bacon.
2. When shanks are well sealed and onion and bacon cooked, add in water, wine, 2 tomatoes chopped, bayleaf, thyme, tomato paste.
3. Roast at 150ºC in a fan forced oven for 1 1/2 hours.
4. Take lamb out and rest for half an hour before slicing off bone, leaving the remaining mixture to continue baking. Add whole tomato.
5. Strain sauce and place back in pan on stovetop. Combine 1 tbs cornflour with 1/4 cup water to form a paste and add to sauce to reduce and thicken. (Keep whole tomatoes in oven).
6. When sauce is ready, return to simmer.
7. Blanch Cannelloni in simmering water for 1-2 minutes, then drain.
8. Lay a sheet of plastic wrap that has plenty of length on bench, and place cannelloni on top. Spoon in the lamb shank, and then roll up in plastic wrap to enclose well, twisting ends of the plastic wrap.
9. Carefully place the cannelloni into simmering water for a further 2-3 minutes, then drain and remove plastic wrap.
10. Place sauce in the bottom of a bowl, cannelloni on top and roasted tomato with parsley to serve.

Drink with this...

Cabernet Sauvignon

"This classic Cabernet has deep purple colour, boasting aromas of blackcurrant, dark chocolate and vanilla with subtle earthy characters."

Red velvet cake

Ingredients:
250g chopped butter
100g melted white chocolate
2 cups caster sugar
1 cup SR flour
1 cup plain flour
1 tsp vanilla essence
1 cup buttermilk
3 tablespoons red food colouring
1/4 cup cocoa
4 eggs

frosting:
1 cup softened butter
500g marscapone cheese
2 tsp vanilla essence
6 cups icing sugar
200g melted white chocolate

Method:
1. Beat butter and sugar.
2. Add the eggs one at a time.
3. Add vanilla essence and cocoa slowly.
4. Slowly add the melted chocolate.
5. Combine the red colouring and the buttermilk in a jug and add to the mix.
6. Slowly add flour.
7. Place 1/4 mixture in small cake tin 8 inches wide.
8. Bake for 175°C in a fan forced oven for 20 minutes or until skewer comes out clean. Repeat until all mixture is cooked and you have four individual cakes.
9. When cooled, wrap in plastic wrap and place in freezer. (This will make it easier to ice).
10. Beat butter and cream cheese for frosting. Add vanilla essence and chocolate and then slowly add icing sugar. Ice each layer, the top and sides. Is best served around room temperature to enjoy the velvet texture.

Drink with this...

Vintage Port

"Displaying a bright purple red colour with a lifted nose of vanilla bean, blackberry and mulberry jam characters that persist in the mouth."

Rings of butterfly pork

Ingredients:
2 butterfly pork steaks
2 asparagus sticks
60g camembert
salt
white pepper
4 slices prosciutto thinly sliced
3 tablespoons olive oil
1 teaspoon sweet Hungarian paprika
1 clove garlic crushed

sauce:
1 granny smith apple
1/2 cup frozen cranberries
2 tsp sugar

Method:
1. Peel apple and cut into quarters, halve each quarter. Put in saucepan with 1 cup boiling water, sugar and cranberries. Boil, reduce and mash. Strain, place back in pan ready to heat and serve with meal.
2. Carefully press and roll out butterfly steaks. Take each asparagus stick and press 30g camembert along the stick.
3. Season with salt and pepper and wrap each asparagus stick with two pieces of prosciutto by rolling them up to help keep the cheese encapsulated. Place in pork and roll into one long log.
4. Tie in bows with cooking string (once at each end and another two times along the steak).
5. In a hot pan, place 1-2 tablespoons of oil mixed with chilli and garlic.
6. Baste the steaks in the chilli oil and pan fry, turning to ensure all the pork is cooked, continually basting.
7. Stand for a few minutes, then undo the string bows.
8. With a sharp knife, cut the ends off and slice three portions (keep the steak together until all is cut or cheese will run out).
9. Arrange on plate and serve with sauce.

Drink with this...
Chardonnay

"A lovely crisp wine, elegant and bristling with tropical fruit flavours. Not heavily oaked so it's great for drinking chilled, on its own. It's also worth trying with fresh fish and grilled chicken salads."

Lamb married with sweet pepper

Ingredients:
1 x 1kg mini lamb roast
2 red capsicums
2 tomatoes
1 red onion diced
2 large garlic cloves
1 tsp sugar

cheese crisp:
50g tasty cheese

mash:
1/4 cup cream
2 large potatoes
75g butter

pea puree:
1 1/2 cup peas
1/2 cup cream
salt
cracked black pepper

Method:
1. Set fan forced oven at 240°C and roast garlic, tomato and capsicums for 20 minutes or until skin blisters on capsicums.
2. Peel off skin on tomatoes and capsicums and squeeze out roasted garlic and mash together with a fork.
3. Place 25g butter in a hot pan, and saute diced onion. Remove onion from pan and mix with capsicum mash and add sugar, salt and pepper to taste.
4. Place another 25g butter in same pan and seal lamb well.
5. Coat lamb with capsicum mash and roast in a fan forced oven at 160°C for 50 minutes. Take out of oven and rest for 2-3 hours. Then return to oven for 30 minutes to heat through.
6. Steam pealed potatoes, add salt, 25g butter, 1/4 cup cream and mash.
7. Grate cheese and spread loosely into two oval shapes on a tray lined with baking paper and place in oven for 3-6 minutes at 160°C.
8. Use a spatula to help to remove the cheese from the tray and mould into desired shape.
9. Boil peas until tender, drain and place in blender with cream and season with salt and pepper. Strain.
10. Slice lamb into thick steaks, top with mash and cheese crisp, and serve with pea puree.

Drink with this...
Shiraz

"Full bodied and very smooth. It's brimming with juicy black and red berry fruit flavours with a hint of warm spice and vanilla... a wine perfect for full flavoured dishes."

White wedding cake

Ingredients:
90g melted white chocolate
60g melted butter
1/4 cup milk
1/4 cup caster sugar
1/2 tsp vanilla essence
1 egg
1 tbs SR flour
3/4 cup plain flour

icing:
180g melted chocolate
1/4 cup cream
3/4 cup icing sugar

Method:
1. Mix all ingredients for cake together. Grease and line a small 10cm square tin with baking paper and bake in a fan forced oven at 120°C for 35-40 minutes, or until a skewer comes out clean.
2. Set cake aside to cool. Wrap in plastic and freeze cake, to make it easier to ice.
3. Melt chocolate in a heatproof bowl over simmering water, and stir through cream.
4. Place in mix master and slowly add icing sugar, beating until the mixture is well combined, thick and pale in colour.
5. Ice cake and decorate with ribbon and your own wedding cake decorations.

Drink with this...

Vintage Port

"Displaying a bright purple red colour with a lifted nose of vanilla bean, blackberry and mulberry jam characters that persist in the mouth."

Andrew Peace wines

The Australian good life bottled

A quarter of a century on from planting its first block, Andrew Peace Wines remains a proud family business and one of the largest family owned wineries in Australia.

What started as a weekend escape transformed into a family passion. Through much toil of three Peace generations, the 'country retreat' vineyard produced its first vintage in 1995 and a commercial winery was born.

Every vintage since has accompanied another chapter of family life - celebrations, milestones and happy memories.

Andrew Peace remains the winemaker today and invites you to enjoy the fruits of the family toil with the same joy they have had in creating it.

Entree:

Roasted champagne oysters	8
Rosette of fish	14
Love all the thyme in Vienna with roasted garlic & fetta	20
Fettish salad	30
Sweet pepper lamb tart	36
Zucchini cakes & flower salad	42
Hommus sweet hommus	52
Soup of pomme d'amour	58
Crouton heart with poached egg	64
Zucchini flowers with bacon & fetta	74
Lovers' heart terrine	80
Avocado & a Roma Tomato	86
Lamb rosettes with date paste	98
Cupid's arrow of sugar and spice beef	104
Rings of Butterfly pork	110

Main:

Parcel of chicken & champagne	10
Quail in a bed of roses	16
In love with fish & chips	22
Hearty chicken with potato rose	32
Bow-tie pasta with amoroso tomato	38
Duck a la rose	44
Hearty pie	54
Moussaka with pomme d'amour	60
Beef cutlet with red rose & wine jus	66
Chilli lovers' chicken	76
Honeyglazed spatchcock	82
Heart & soul cakes	88
Date with Moroccan lamb	100
Lamb shank in cannelloni	106
Lamb married with sweet pepper	112

Dessert:

Champagne & flowers sorbet	12
Poached pears in champagne	18
Golden syrup love dumplings	24
Fruit of passion meringue	34
Melted heart chocolate pudding	40
Champagne & white chocolate mousse	46
Sweetie pie	56
Lovers' chocolate fondue for two	62
Chantilly kisses for a king	68
Sweet heart cheese cake	78
French kissed raspberries	84
Tia Maria & dark chocolate icecream	90
Date pudding	102
Red velvet cake	108
White wedding cake	114

Summer menu	7
Autumn menu	29
Winter menu	51
Spring menu	73
Special occasion menu	96

With thanks to

Andrew Peace Wines
PO Box 92
4077 Murray Valley Highway
Piangil, Victoria, AUSTRALIA, 3597
www.apwines.com
Ph: 613 5030 5291
Fax: 613 5030 6120

Wild Hibiscus Flower Company
PO Box 17, Windsor, New South Wales
AUSTRALIA 2756
www.wildhibiscus.com